THIS BOOK IS LOVINGLY DISTRIBUTED BY

Lionheart Ministry

All book purchases bless Lionheart Ministry.
To receive complimentary copies of this book and to learn more about
how to receive future creations visit **Lionheartministry.com**

Thankful for...

MY HUSBAND JONATHAN

Thank you for encouraging me to keep creating and to not give up on God-sized dreams. You are one of the most generous people I've ever known and I love you with my whole heart.

EDITOR

Rachel Dube
Your steadfast giftings and faithfulness as
my sister and friend.

TO MY CHILDREN

I stand in awe of the love of Jesus inside both of you. I am the most proud and thankful mother in the entire world. You both shine Jesus' love to me and the world.

GRAPHIC ARTIST

Kayla Follin
kaylafollin.com
Your kindness and creative wonders weaved
in and through the pages.

ARTIST

Lynne Hudson
lynnehudson.com
Thank for your heavenly art, prayers,
Godly love and inspiration!

All content and rights are reserved and cannot be
used without written consent.

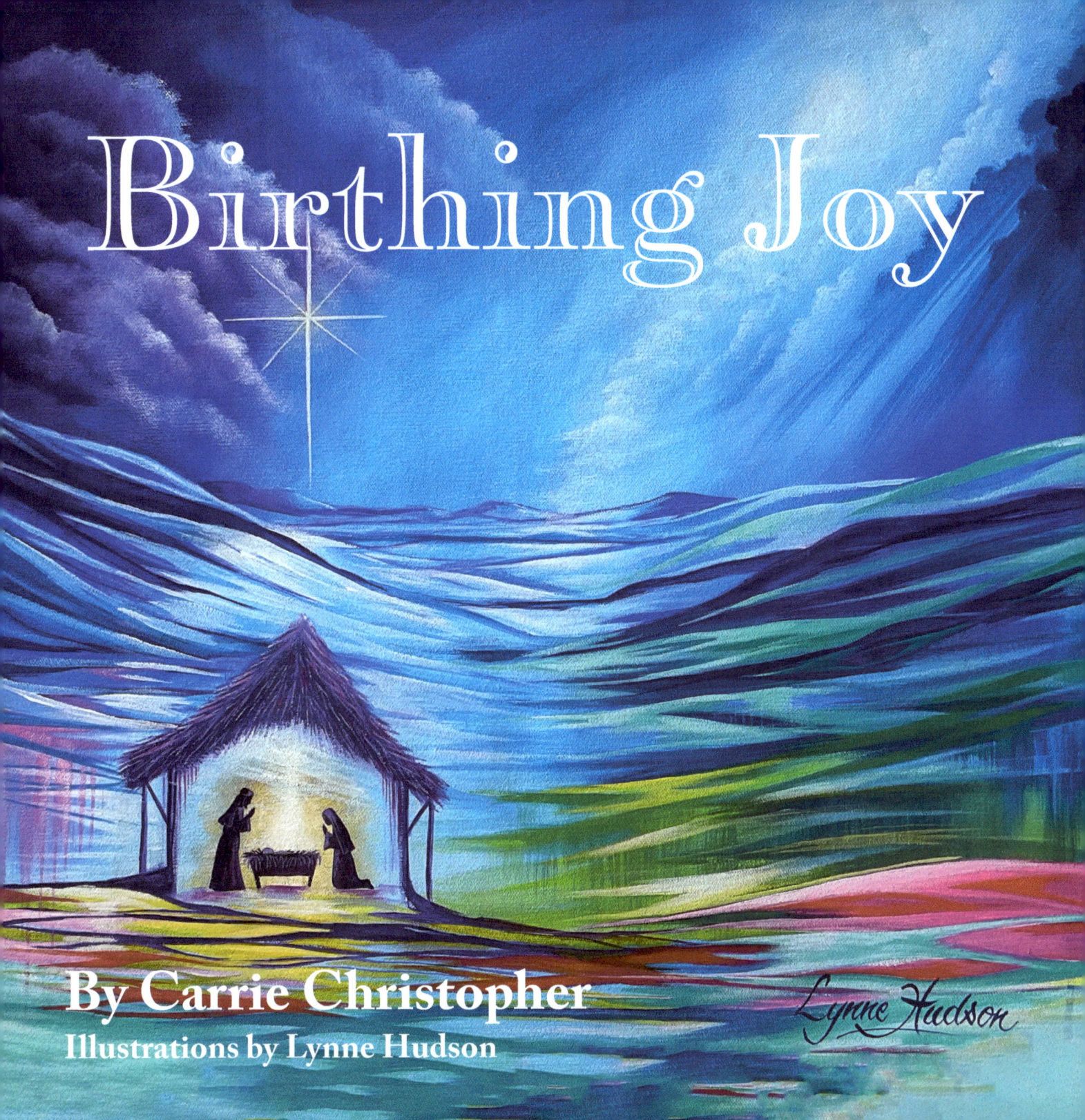

Son of God

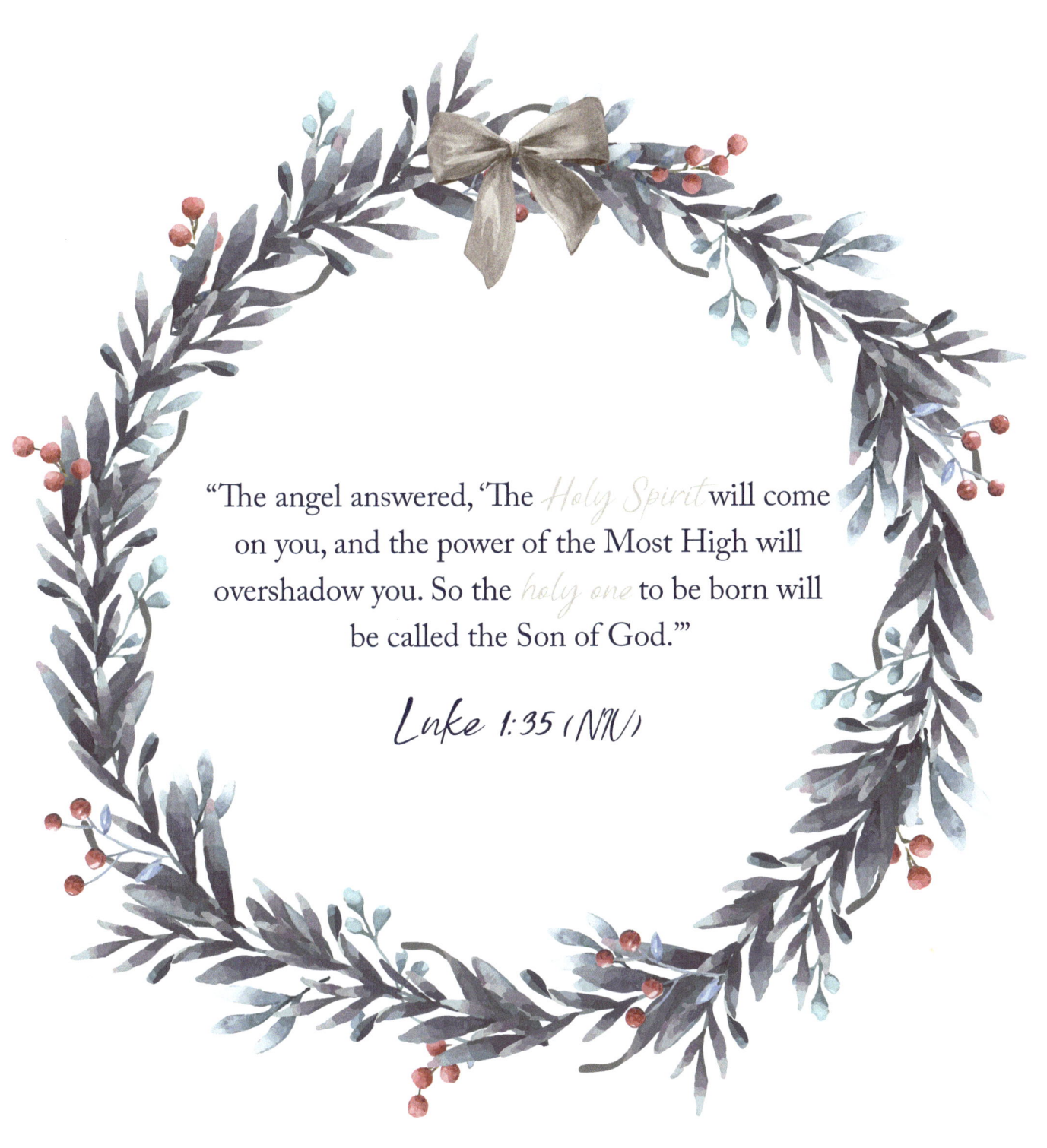

"The angel answered, 'The *Holy Spirit* will come on you, and the power of the Most High will overshadow you. So the *holy one* to be born will be called the Son of God.'"

Luke 1:35 (NIV)

Merry and bright,
it was the perfect starry night

Where the shepherds were led,
guided by the bright star ahead

Cataclysmic grace would birth
His bright, holy, *perfect face*

Miracles from heaven were sent,
where now and forevermore every
knee would be bent

Staring into the night, she labored
and held her perfect babe lovingly tight

Through this very intimate birth,
God sent his victorious love to
empower the earth

A gift to us so great, radically changing
earth's fate, offered to each and to all,
undoing the evil of the Fall

His love now giving us life and cancelling
our debt that caused so much strife

Our King, our King ushered in salvation,
causing our hearts to rejoice and sing

A healer, a hoper, a planner,
a King that would carry a redemptive banner

A banner of love, peace, joy, and grace,
to anyone who would long to look
into His face

A face full of *kindness, mercy, and love,*
God's greatest gift sent from heaven above

Jesus, our Christmas, entered earth in a
tangible way, so we can celebrate access to
salvation, each and every day

Love came down as a gift, to heal sin
and Satan's wayward rift

Have you opened the gift of Christ's
infusing love that was sent for you
from heaven above?

A gift of wonder for you to share, ROYAL,
righteous robes that are yours to wear

Receive, receive, child of man; it is the Lord
who speaks over your sin, the Great I Am

From our family to yours, may the
Lord Jesus open to you heavens doors!

Our Deliverer

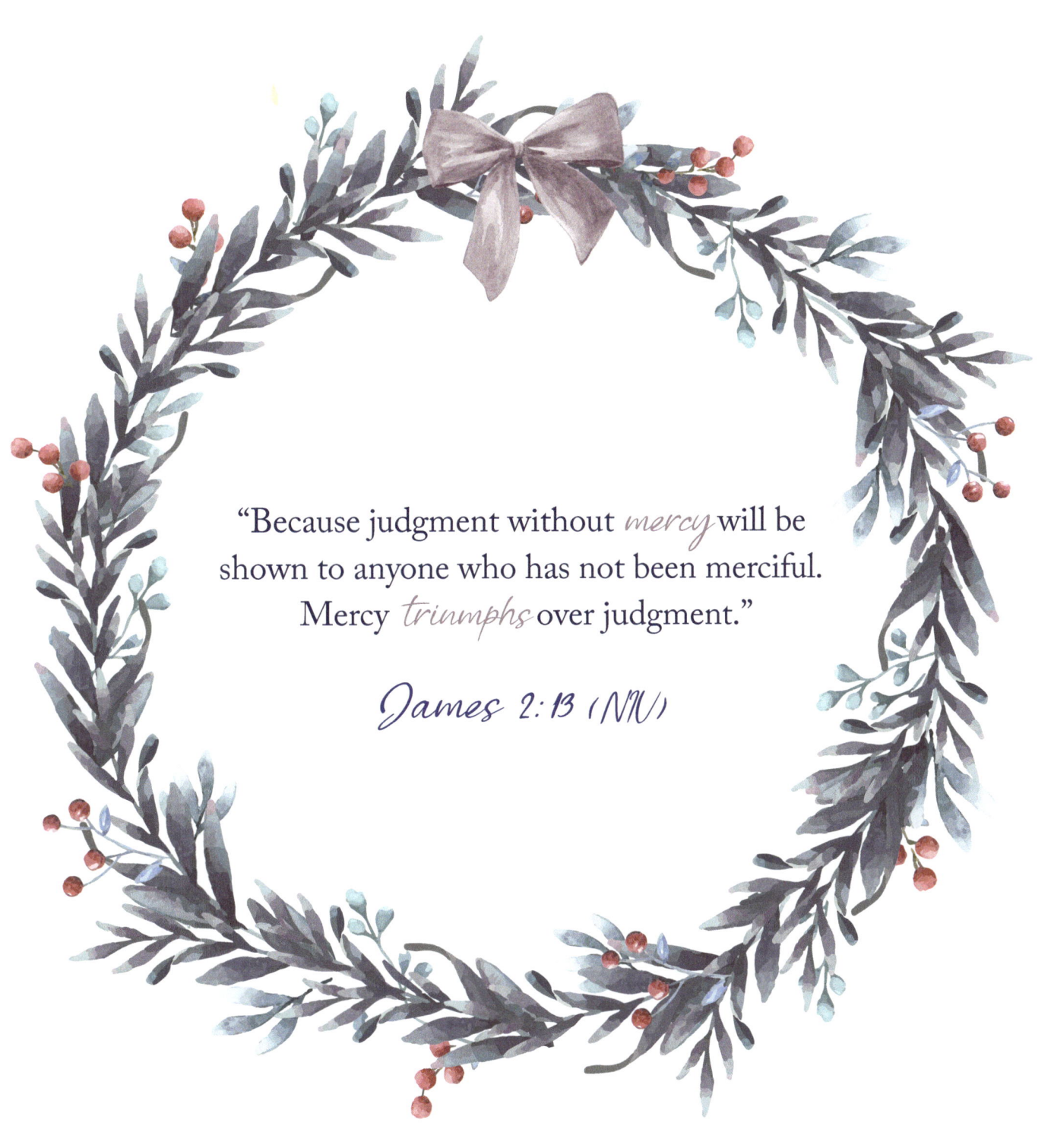

Stiff, unwelcome, repellant, angry, wound inflicting, selfish pride; an *accumulating* lack of love lingers through the air. Hostility, unforgiveness, lust, rage; faithlessness remains stagnantly producing an aroma of confusion and fear, creating a mirror image of darkness. The darkness begins to tear down and ravage hearts. Pure chaos forms from this entity of lovelessness. Our hearts are shriveling, stuck, gasping continually for breath, for life. Man without love dies inwardly. As the inward, *all-encompassing* anguish churns with hopelessness, our physical bodies suffocate, not connected to an essential lifeline. Hunger aches and travails. Lack of love weakens, destroys and eventually kills.

But to be loved feels like an aroma of intoxicating flowers, feels like the gentle wind blowing towards us on a hot summer day, feels like a forever warm embrace of peace that wraps around our anxiety. Cocooned and consumed in pure bliss, joy fills us with an *unwavering* delight. Love fills every ounce of our hungry being with everlasting perfection. A love like this holds us intimately close, nourishing our dry bones and our weary souls, transforming us from one degree of glory to another. This love, the one *true love,* fills us to the point of overflowing. This trail of love flows like a heavenly wind, touching those around us with divine tastes of abundance.

What love is this that can be so supernaturally encompassing?

It is the love of the Savior, who yearns for nothing more than to hold us in His perfect love. He earnestly desires to be with us in the dark, illuminating the walls of our hearts, *awakening* us to the one true love that will never fail us. The character of Christ is marked by a faithful, unrelenting, *glory-filled* desire to be with us and love us perfectly and wholly. It is a love that touched down as a small babe, born in a manger, and now awakens the world on Christmas morning with hope and a declaration of promised victory. This glory is meant to be pondered on, wondered about, and received. The *glory of Love* came for me and came for you. May you and yours feel, taste, and touch the wondrous love of Jesus as your ultimate gift, saturating your home this season with the aroma of hope.

Jesus

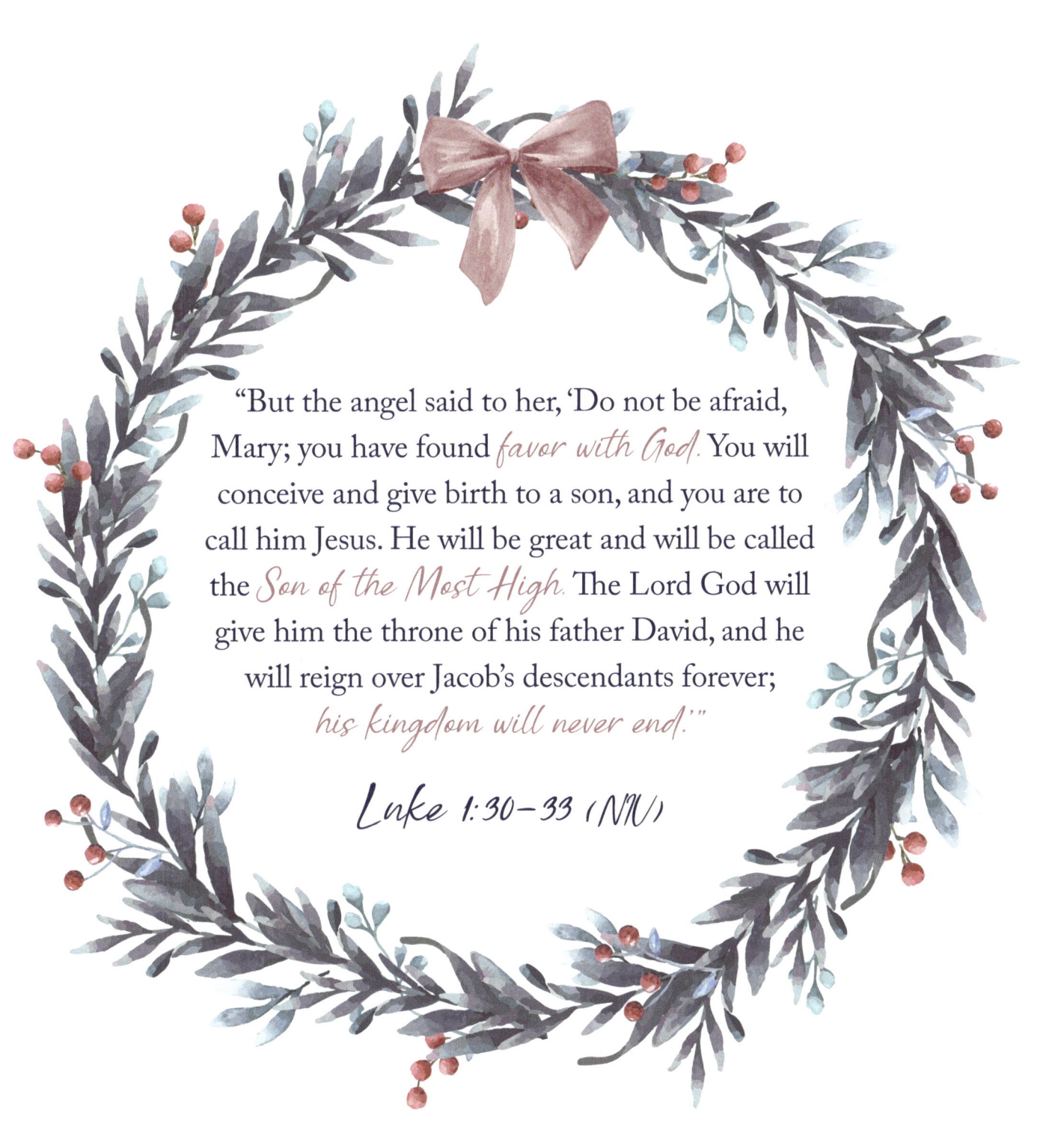

"But the angel said to her, 'Do not be afraid, Mary; you have found *favor with God*. You will conceive and give birth to a son, and you are to call him Jesus. He will be great and will be called the *Son of the Most High*. The Lord God will give him the throne of his father David, and he will reign over Jacob's descendants forever; *his kingdom will never end.'"*

Luke 1:30–33 (NIV)

Singing ringing from the abode of heaven. Angelic presences flooding the earth with celebration, encouraging Mary and Joseph to continue on the rough trail of travel.

Shepherds, anointed, *declaring* a celebration, came from the rugged fields into a whole new beginning.

Kings, preparing, with gifts of great wealth, set their eyes upon the bright, looming star that led them onward.

A miracle was assigned to manifest at an appointed time, an immaculate conception to be birthed. Awake in the stable, Mary and Joseph prepared to host the presence and the *earth shaking awakening* of life's redemptive King.

A babe entered, bringing redemption, an explosion of the heavenlies landed triumphantly; all hope was wrapped up in a tiny child's entrance.

Hope came through God, who was made into flesh, to prosper the land in ferocious love.

Love makes His way into the hearts of man by *becoming one of us,* so we do not have to be separated from God the Father.

The wrapping of His love is a gift that cannot be sent back. It must be embraced, for the survival of humanity rests on this little one's life. All of the earth groans at the sight of His face.

His face has witnessed every weapon of the enemy, seen every heart of man, holds every breath of knowledge, and was created by the intentional *Word of the Father.*

He was sent down for us, for me and you, in the form of a baby boy.

Mary sat in the illuminated darkness, embracing her gift from heaven, her baby boy, the greatest treasure ever known to mankind, the Savior of the entire world.

He is the one that would look at the face of death and laugh at the attempts of the enemy's schemes.

He is the one that has defeated sin and death through the coming of His infancy, His entrance into humanity. Our God was willing to *humble* himself to the point of death on a cross, bearing what we couldn't, our sin and our shame.

The babe would grow into the offshoot, the root of Jesse, into a *rich saving grace,* for the sin that has entangled His people.

The gift of Christ's life is the greatest treasure. Would you choose to embrace the thoughts of God toward you on this Christmas morning?

Would you choose to hold the babe of wonder in your arms, pondering and praising, experiencing the *awe and wonder,* tasting the barnyard bliss, with the expectation of revival?

This child doesn't stay as a babe, no; He rules and reigns over the nations!

This Christmas season, set aside your time, in pure devotion, to treasure and ponder the work of a King's miracle.

Which kingdom do you choose, your own or His? Would you allow this gift of Christ's presence WITH US to change you, to allow your life be filled with bounties of the Spirit and *blessings of His love?*

Or would you shun the risen God who wants to take up residence within your soul, to nourish you, strengthen you, and give you new life that would save your soul from the depths of hell?

The bells are ringing, *Christ has come.* May Christ birth in your soul the satisfying fruits of His presence and existence, here and today, redeeming you and letting out the majestic exposition of His heart of love, pouring onto the nations His hope, peace, joy, and love.

Our Savior

Mighty Connselor

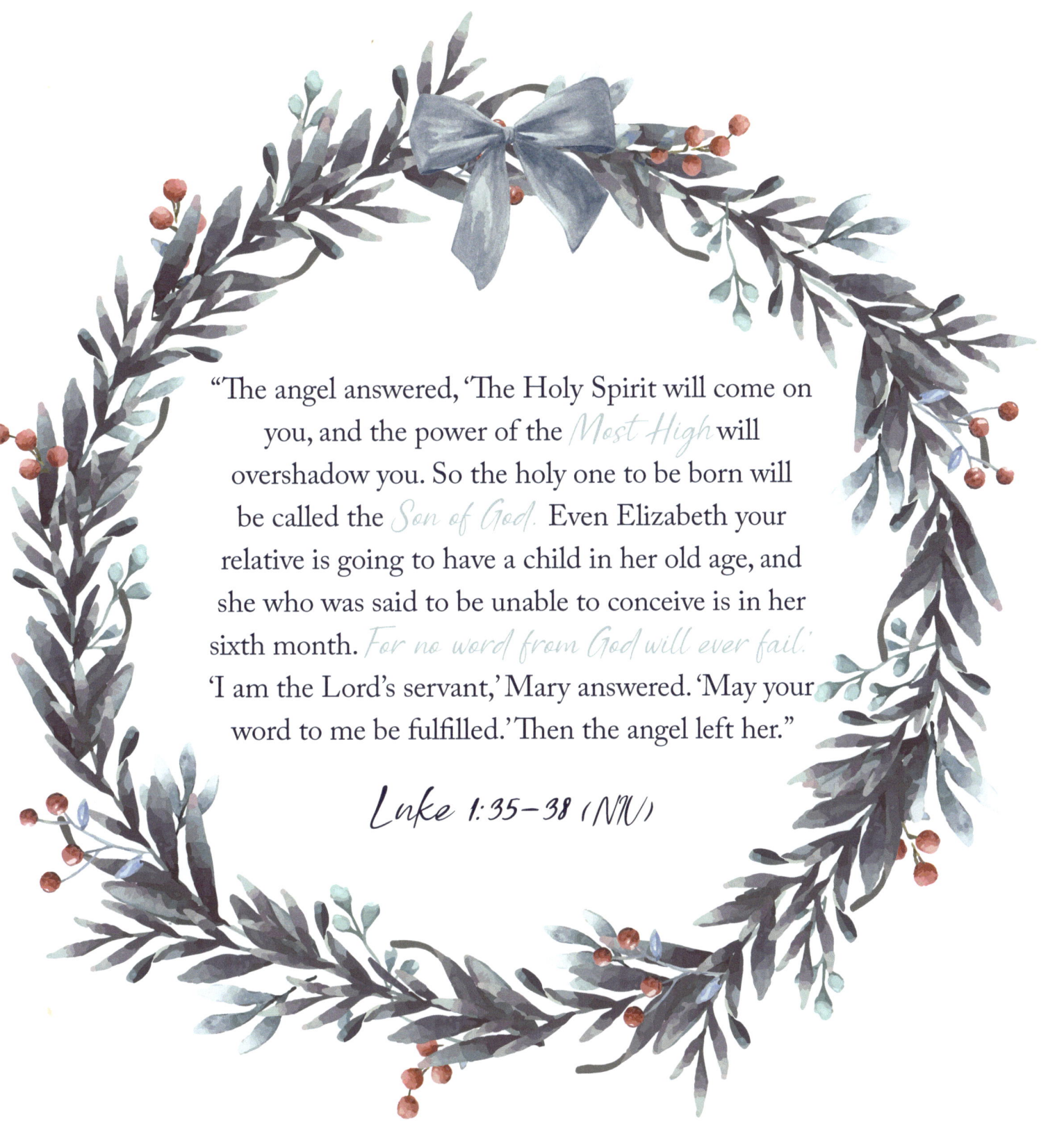

"The angel answered, 'The Holy Spirit will come on you, and the power of the *Most High* will overshadow you. So the holy one to be born will be called the *Son of God.* Even Elizabeth your relative is going to have a child in her old age, and she who was said to be unable to conceive is in her sixth month. *For no word from God will ever fail.*' 'I am the Lord's servant,' Mary answered. 'May your word to me be fulfilled.' Then the angel left her."

Luke 1:35–38 (NIV)

Evoked by love and awoken by love, came the baby boy, Jesus, for each and for all.

Tears streamed down Mary's face in joy, in expression of the trials that she has endured in the long journey.

Her heart, her life, her *redemption,* were willingly and obediently set aside for the birthing of Christ within her.

Fear didn't hold her back as she welcomed the *miraculous,* as she reveled in conversations with angels.

A womb explosion of grace-filled, tender care, reaching as high as the heavenlies, invaded earth.

Heaven was coming. *God had made a way.*

Songs of praises and gratitude reached all who stared into the eyes of the brightly lit face of joy that entered the manger that day.

Even the animals bowed; the cobwebs shook in trembling and fear; the enemy of our lives hid, wailing at the doomed destruction set apart for him through the ushering in of Christ.

It was over; it was done. Christ's birth had invaded earth with a *kiss of grace,* an embrace of holy, soothing love, and a wave of overflowing redemption.

Would you join me in holding in your heart the expression of God's love, *faithfulness,* and tender care this Christmas season?

The gift of salvation, a tangible relationship restored, was brought through the unfathomable lowliness of Jesus being birthed in a manger.

Reach, reach for the *star of Christ* which led the wise men along. Smell the aroma of Christ filling the air, giving us, as His children, laughter and delight in the face of the accuser.

The gift is yours if you will dare to open HIM.

His heart opens wide, exploding the overwhelming, audacious, *assertive love* of God for you, for me, and for yours.

He came to declare to each and to all that God has made a bridge to redemption, love, joy, hope, and peace.

The flourishing of the root of Jesse prevails and invades the stinging death of sin within us, accomplishing *peace* that we could never obtain.

Would you receive this *gift of Christ* this Christmas season?

As a Christian, would you reignite, and re-esteem the very presence of God with you in this season?

If you are in an estranged relationship with God, would you be brought into a new birth, a new heavenly realm of salvation, *a new relationship* with the Holy God of Israel who wants to cradle YOU with His love?

The only way up is down in humility.

This season, we kneel in *reverence* to a Holy God, who came in infancy so we could receive eternity.

Humbly witness and herald a Merry Christmas.

Lamb of God

Prince of Peace

"Love and *faithfulness* meet together; *righteousness* and *peace* kiss each other.

Psalm 85:10 (NIV)

Sentiments of Christ are flowing, richly and vastly over the land —

Sentiments of His love, *propelling His glorious Church* forward

A display of encounters that are far beyond our earthly pleasures

Sentiments of His riches are given with a cost

But are birthed with *His love*

Sentiments of His love are speaking, expressions, alive and active through His Word

Piercing our hearts with confession, repentance, and *overflowing grace*

Sentiments of His grace are pouring in immense purposes

Unstoppable, unquenchable, fiery Holy Spirit access to Him

A God who came to be with us through the ushering in of *His heavenly birth*

A God who advanced past the kingdom troops of opposition

A Lord who lavished *His great love* upon you, me and us

Speaking a word of freedom to the multitudes

Anyone who would touch His cloak would be *brought to His heart*

His heart sent from heaven above

Sentiments of His sacred offering of death

The nails piercing His hands and attempting to stifle his love

A love that could never be stifled- a love that could far outlast our own

A love that would fight until death and be resurrected in *triumph* from the permanence of a grave

Grace fought for us the day that awakened baby Jesus to earth

Grace and mercy defeated the spirits of the darkness and brought glory's light

Awakened to glory's light were Mary and Joseph and generations beyond

Heaven's song came to earth as angels heralded His great entrance

The earth split open that day, revealing its callused core

Welcoming a Savior to speak on behalf of His sheep

Whispering hope, joy, peace, and love

Streaming from His face, *a bright glow,* beaming with heavenly riches

A baby full of heaven's wealth, making His permanent abode in the hearts of man

The mind of Christ upon us, filling His Church with *excellence, dominion, His presence,* and *power*

Sentiments streaming from heaven above

Wonderful Counselor

Immannel – God With Us

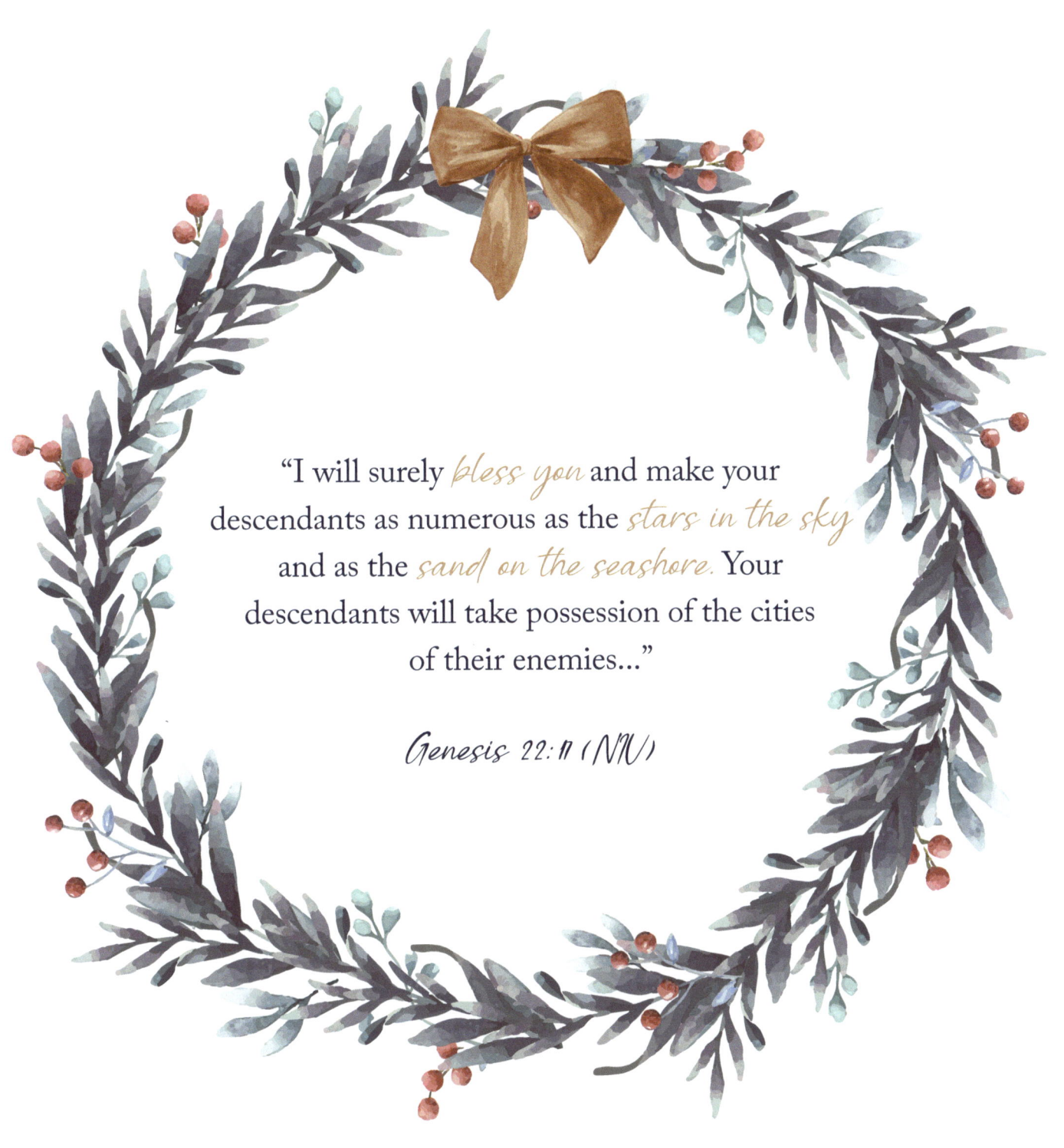

"I will surely *bless you* and make your descendants as numerous as the *stars in the sky* and as the *sand on the seashore*. Your descendants will take possession of the cities of their enemies..."

Genesis 22:11 (NIV)

The body of Christ resembles stars in a dark sky

Where warriors run and fight, soaring high

Where one *lays down his life,* willingly prepared to die

Where miracles happen and His children, basked in freedom, fly

Where His stars *shimmer brightly* and His holy light glows

Drawing others near to this miracle, and the Spirit flows

A generation, *redeemed,* a flock now led

Birthed by our Savior, continuously fed

Nourished, *strengthened,* and propelled into glory light

Came Jesus that morning, sending darkness to flight

Stars now beaming, His disciples running in power

Giving grace to all people, allowing them to flower

Glimmering glory, the night sky is filled in *great wonder*

Jesus born to send darkness to be visually sundered

Mighty God

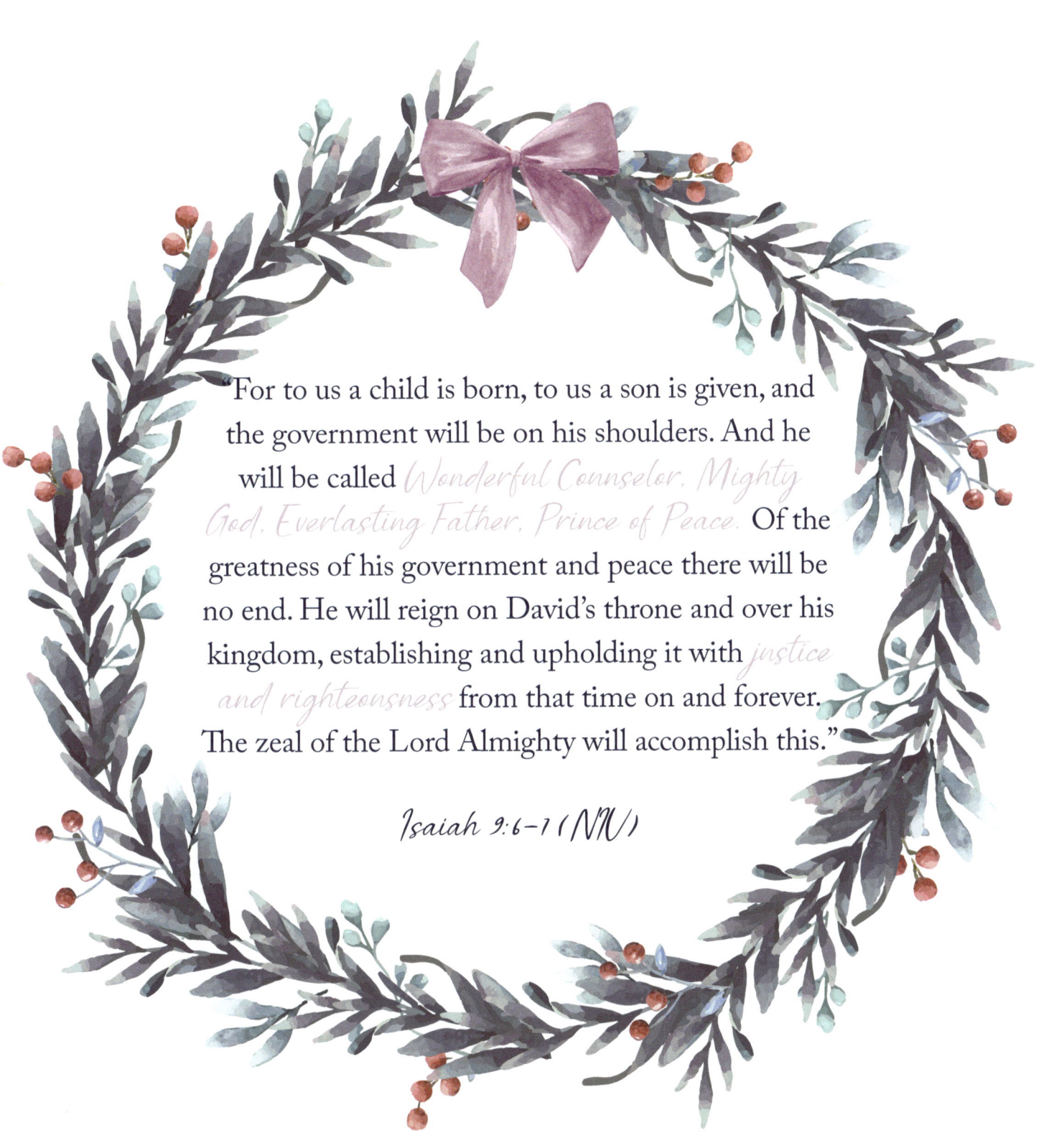

A mother's heart

Beholding deep joy

Her mind fixed on the *miracles of creation*

Woven, crafted, designed for great glory

Unfathomable riches carried in her womb

Encountering grace as she gazed into His bright eyes

The heavens exploded with triumph

Waves billowing as *helms of healing* for the nations

The long-awaited Messiah

An embodied grace in human form

Gushing *glory and triumphant* tunes

Heralding His entrance of dominion

Sweet mercy divinely touched down to earth

Torrents of darkness sweeping in opposition, shaking in fear at the *power of light*

Trusted truths released at the entrance of His birth

Birthing joy, now married with hope

A hope unrelenting, grace providing, love abiding, the *presence of God with us*

He entered into our darkness so we could experience His radically radiant light

Stars beamed proudly as they ushered shepherds into the heavenly promise of Abraham

Generations now passed from that founding father prophecy

And yet His perfect timing carried fruit-filled awakenings

No longer slaves, *we are promised freedom*

Christmas marks a carrying of Christ's love into our lives

Leading us onward with singing, saving grace

Joy released into the heavenlies as Mary birthed *eternal joy*

The joy of our salvation has been given life, access, and longevity through His coming

Wonderful Counselor, Mighty God, Everlasting Father, *Prince of Peace*

Everlasting Father

"We love because *he first loved us.*"

1 John 4:19 (NIV)

Love divine

Came to shine

Love awoke as *glory spoke*

Love released

That would never cease

Love spoke what sin broke

Love shook what the enemy took

Love *abolished the Law*

So grace is all we saw

Love cascading

Mercy unfading

Love came near

So all could hear

Love was carried

Through humble Mary

Love flowed

Salvation showed

Through His birth, grace and glory wildly collide

Unrelenting love would pursue us so there's no reason to hide

Angelic *celebration* awaited as humanity, in our desperation, groaned

It was God in the flesh, sent to earth, *generously and joyfully loaned*

Living Light

"The light shines in the darkness, and the darkness has not overcome it."

John 1:5 (NIV)

How was it possible

That Jesus could leave the love of the Father?

How is it true

That He came for shamed sinners
and would even bother?

How can it be

That a King would leave His throne
for you and for me?

How is it so

Despite the gnarling opposition,
that He would even go?

How did it feel

Knowing that His very own blood would
be the only way for us to heal?

How can it be

That He came through immaculate conception—

Surpassing all humankind understandings and perceptions?

How did He wait

All the hundreds of years in between,
determining our feeble fate?

How much did He love us?

With a willingness displayed

Through his birth, sacrifice, and the death
that His grace actively dismayed

He came for sinners, full of shame and pride

Born in a manger, and on a tear stained cross

He willingly died

See His gesture, hear His voice and His call

Submit your hearts and with humility,
willingly fall

The invitation of *soul healing* awaits
until you fully open

The presence of His power,
all the riches He has spoken

A gift so expressive, *brimming and bright*

A gift birthed in the dark of Mary's night

A gift given of spiritual sight

In the midst of our desperation and fearful plight

A healing, a telling, *a salvation so bold*

Willing to release to all who
would graciously hold

Forces of evil tried to thwart

The blessing that our babe, Jesus, sought to court

Bringing *justice, salvation, and peace*

Releasing an invitation of love
that would never cease

Come and gaze at what this season speaks

Grace pouring out to hearts that are meek

Open your hand, *surrender your heart*

God's radical love poured down on
you is just the start

Fall in love with your protective king

And joyfully accept His covenant ring

He came for *me, for you, and for all*

The melodic music of Christmas heralds
His holy call

Our Rock

Our Redeemer

"A new command I give you: Love one another. As I have loved you, so you must love one another. By this everyone will know that you are my disciples, if you love one another."

John 13:34-35 (NIV)

A gathering of families joining together in unity

A cohesive Church being birthed through the *birth of Christ*

He came into the flesh so we could be a body, together

Loving graciously as *He loved us*

Lights flicker and glimmer, looped and weaved through the depths of greenery, hugging the Christmas tree with splendor

Lighting up the darkness of the night with a profound glittering and twinkling from His eyes, the *light of the nations* came as a beacon of hope to the perishing

Smells of jubilee rise in the air, Christmas fragrances of pine, balsam, and cooking permeate our senses

Frankincense and myrrh display the gifts of celebration, as kings come and bow down to the only true Savior of the world. These aromas awaken the world to the miracle of a babe who came in humility, birthed in a manger

Gifts under the tree, piled high, building anticipation and excitement, marking a *joyous celebration*

The one true gift of Christ comes through the impossible, giving the earth a tangible expression of love

A gift of salvation shook the world with *divinity, power and glory* on display. Ready to be opened by those ready to receive.

Christmas melodies spoken, written, and cherished in great wonder, filling the air with triumphant tunes, notes of freedom ring!

The angelic entrance of heavenly celebration cascades over the entirety of man with *joy, peace, and praise, heralding goodness.* A Savior has come.

www.ingramcontent.com/pod-product-compliance
Lightning Source LLC
Chambersburg PA
CBHW041407010526
44107CB00015B/1099